Oxford Primary Social Studies

Growing Together

3

Pat Lunt

OXFORD
UNIVERSITY PRESS

Contents

Unit 1 Culture and identity   3

1.1	Who am I?	4
1.2	What can I offer?	6
1.3	Personal goals	8
1.4	Functions of the family	10
1.5	Roles within the family	12
1.6	Cultural heritage	14
1.7	Celebrating local culture	16
1.8	Cultures living together	18
	Review questions	20

Unit 2 History and heritage   21

2.1	Historical evidence	22
2.2	Evidence for local history	24
2.3	Early history	26
2.4	Early tribes and trade	28
	Review questions	30

Unit 3 People and places   31

3.1	Climate	32
3.2	Climate and human activity	34
3.3	Using local maps	36
3.4	Locations within a country	38
3.5	Regions	40
3.6	Natural coastal features	42
3.7	Inland physical features	44
3.8	Physical features and water	46
3.9	Mapping physical features	48
3.10	Natural resources	50
3.11	The Arabian Gulf	52
3.12	Changing the environment	54
3.13	Transport	56
3.14	Populations	58
3.15	People and places	60
3.16	Where people live	62
	Review questions	64

Unit 4 Citizenship   65

4.1	Being a part of society	66
4.2	A multicultural society	68
4.3	Using natural resources	70
4.4	Using public spaces	72
4.5	The school environment	74
4.6	School resources	76
4.7	How do we communicate?	78
4.8	Means of communication	80
4.9	Social groups and rules	82
4.10	Public services 1	84
4.11	Public services 2	86
4.12	Employment	88
4.13	Consumers	90
	Review questions	92

Unit 5 Health and wellbeing   93

5.1	Food and health	94
5.2	Exercise and health	96
5.3	Staying safe at school	98
5.4	Healthy relationships	100
	Review questions	102

| | Glossary | 103 |

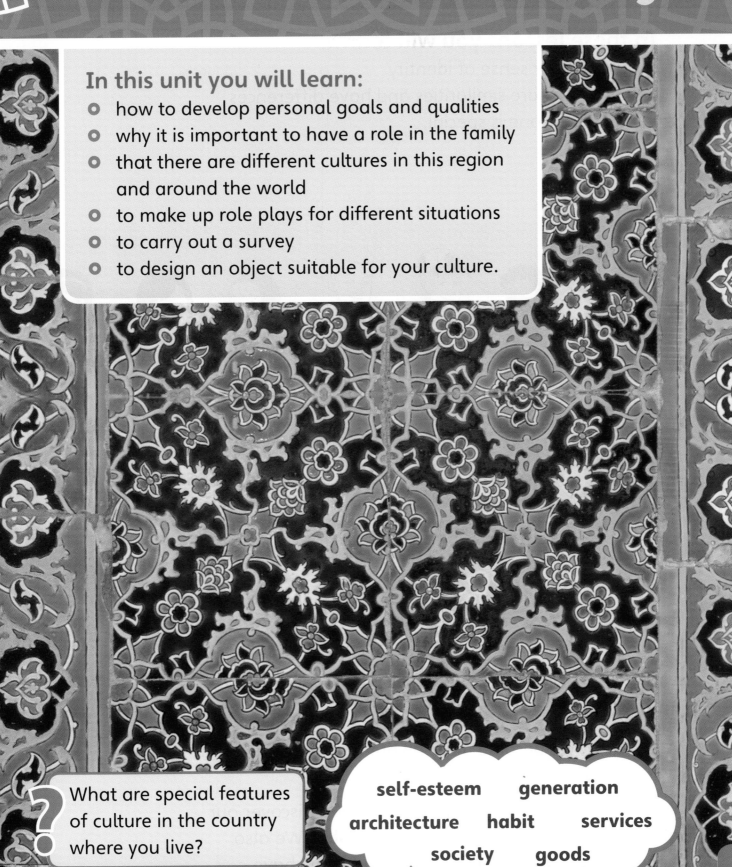

1 Culture and identity

In this unit you will learn:

- how to develop personal goals and qualities
- why it is important to have a role in the family
- that there are different cultures in this region and around the world
- to make up role plays for different situations
- to carry out a survey
- to design an object suitable for your culture.

? What are special features of culture in the country where you live?

self-esteem   generation
architecture   habit   services
society   goods

1.1 Who am I?

In these lessons you will learn:

- about your sense of identity
- that we share similarities and have differences
- that everyone is special.

Identity

▲ We know we are unique because we all look different.

Each person has a body. This is the physical part of who a person is.

Each person is more than just a body.

Each of us is a separate person. We can think and feel.

As we grow we become more aware of who we are and what we are like.

We begin to develop likes and dislikes. We discover our gifts and talents. We develop a personality. We also begin to form an identity. This is the idea we have about who we are.

Forming an identity

Many things help us develop our identity. The groups to which we belong probably have the biggest influence.

One of the most important groups is our family.

Other important groups are friendship groups and groups inside and outside school.

Other things help form our identity such as the country we come from, the race we belong to and the beliefs we hold.

We all belong to one big group – the human race.

▲ We form our identity partly because of where we feel we belong.

▲ Part of our identity comes from belonging to the human race.

Activities

1 Work with a partner and make a list of things about both of you that are the same. For example everyone needs water to drink. Then make a list of things that makes you different. Make sure you list something that is special about each of you.

2 Draw a picture of yourself and write about the things that help explain who you are, such as your family, your school, your clubs, what you like and things you are good at.

1.2 What can I offer?

In this lesson you will learn:
- to identify positive personal qualities
- how to develop positive personal qualities.

Learning and growing

As we grow we build up more knowledge about the world.

We can learn new skills that will help us to do particular tasks.

We can also develop our positive personal qualities.

▲ As we grow we learn new skills.

Growing and changing

As we grow we become more aware of ourselves as people.

We are able to think about our characteristics and our personality.

We can identify the things we like about ourselves and the things it would be good to change or improve.

We can practise thinking or behaving in ways that help this.

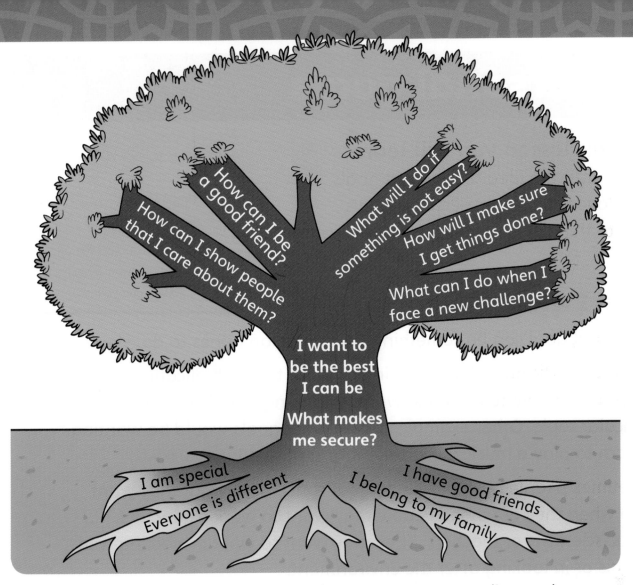

How can I be a good friend?

How can I show people that I care about them?

What will I do if something is not easy?

How will I make sure I get things done?

What can I do when I face a new challenge?

I want to be the best I can be

What makes me secure?

I am special

Everyone is different

I belong to my family

I have good friends

▲ We need strong roots like a tree so that we can stay standing and grow.

Useful habits

If we practise thinking or behaving in a particular way then that way of thinking or behaving becomes a **habit**. If we keep thinking about ourselves and other people in a positive way then that is the way we will naturally think.

If we practise behaving in ways that remember other people's feelings and needs we will become a kind, thoughtful and helpful person.

Activities

1 Draw a picture of a tree like the one above. Write answers to the questions given on the branches on the tree above, like 'I will be loyal to show I am a good friend.'

2 Work in a group to make up role plays that show how people have positive personal qualities in different situations.

1.3 Personal goals

In this lesson you will learn:
- about the idea of personal goals
- to identify some personal goals
- to think of ways to reach those goals.

What I want to do

A personal goal can be something that a person hopes to do.

Personal goals can include wanting to learn the multiplication tables, being able to read and write, or finding out about a particular topic. Other examples of personal goals would be wanting to learn to play a musical instrument or a particular sport.

Sometimes people have a definite goal concerning what they want to do when they are older. People may want to work as doctors, artists, scientists or teachers. They may want to work protecting wild animals or in looking after the environment.

To achieve any of these goals people also have to set some different goals. They have to commit to all the effort of practising skills and gaining knowledge.

▼ Many people have a goal of what they would like to do as an adult.

Who I want to be

A personal goal can also be about how a person wants to be.

A personal goal could be to do with how a person feels about him or herself. Perhaps a person needs to build up their confidence or learn how to deal with difficulties.

A personal goal could be about how well a person relates to other people.

▲ It is good to think about how we can help other people.

Activities

1 Answer these questions for yourself.

- How well do you cope when something is not easy – can you keep going?

- How good are you at telling other people what you think and feel?

- How often do you see what other people need, and do something to help?

- Do you make decisions based on what you know to be right or wrong?

- How easy is it for you to work with other people?

- Are you curious about life? What are the things you want to know and find out about?

- Are you able to respect other people's views in different situations?

2 Discuss the questions in a group to decide why these things are important.

1.4 Functions of the family

In this lesson you will learn:
- about families of different sizes
- about why families are so important.

A family is a group of people who are related to one another.

People can be related by birth, which means that they share lines of parents and grandparents. People can also be related by a special type of relationship, such as marriage.

▲ People in a family live in the same home.

When we talk about a 'family unit' we usually mean the people in a family who live in the same home.

Families are made up of people who are related to one another by birth or through marriage. Our families include parents and their children, who will be brothers and sisters to one another. Families also include grandparents, aunts, uncles, nephews, nieces and cousins.

Why families are important

Families are important because children are born within a family.

A family gives people a sense of belonging. It is an important part of their identity.

This sense of belonging means that all family members want to co-operate to make sure the family is happy and successful.

In a family people feel loved and cared for. People feel safe and are able to develop confidence and **self-esteem**.

◄ Members of a family can support one another in difficult times.

In a family, people learn how to live alongside others. Family members learn how to give and receive support and help.

In a family, parents teach their children about the kind of behaviour that is accepted in **society**. Children learn about their family's **values**, culture and beliefs. They learn about the values that are important in society.

Activities

1 Work as a class to carry out a survey to find out about different family sizes.

2 Write about some of the values you learn within your family and why they are important.

1.5 Roles within the family

In this lesson you will learn:
- about the roles of different people in a family
- about why having a role is important.

Needs within the family

A family has to provide for all the needs of its members. Family members need food, water, clothing and shelter.

◀ A family provides for basic needs such as food.

People in a family need to feel that they are loved and cared for. The family home has to be looked after, and kept clean and safe.

Different members of a family can take on certain roles to make sure that these things happen. Some of the roles and responsibilities can be shared.

Roles within the family

Today the needs of most families are met by one or more people working to earn money. This money is used to buy all the **goods** and **services** a family needs. The family members who earn this money can be one or both parents. Sometimes older children are still living at home when they start work and so they too bring money into the household.

It is good for everyone to share the roles which ensure that a household is kept clean, tidy and is looked after. This helps people to learn about responsibility and about basic life skills.

▲ Today people use money to buy the things they need from markets or shops, as here in Egypt.

◄ If we share a space with other people, we share the responsibility for keeping it clean and tidy.

Everyone in the family has a role in terms of showing love, care and respect.

Activity

In many cultures, the family is completely responsible for providing and cooking food, maintaining a household and keeping it clean and tidy. Below are some of the jobs that need to be done in a household. In a group, decide which members of a family, including children, might be responsible for carrying out each job. Tell the group if you do any of these things and how you are responsible for helping to keep your home clean and tidy.

washing up	washing clothes	washing up	mowing the lawn
tending the garden	mending a tap	watering plants	bathing a baby
putting clothes away	tidying a room	doing the ironing	collecting laundry
dusting	clearing the table	hanging out washing	cooking meals

1.6 Cultural heritage

In this lesson you will learn:
- about how culture is handed down
- why cultural heritage is important.

Culture and heritage

Culture is the mixture of ideas, values and actions shared by a group of people. Culture can be shown in lots of different ways, including through art, music, food, dance, dress and **architecture**.

Cultural heritage is the parts of a culture that are handed on from one **generation** to the next.

Cultural heritage is partly made up of things that you can see and touch, like paintings, objects, buildings and **monuments**.

◄ Even a small piece of tile lets us know how people liked to decorate their buildings in the past.

Cultural heritage is also made up of things that cannot be touched, such as ideas and values, arts like dance and music, and special **rituals**.

▲ An oud is a traditional musical instrument found in many Arab cultures.

In some places a natural feature can be important to the culture. For example, the desert played a big part in forming the nomadic culture of several Arab tribes. In countries of the Arabian Gulf, Islam has a central role in society and influences the culture of those places.

▲ The shrine to Bib Maryam in Oman was built around 1300.

Why cultural heritage is important

Our culture is an important part of our identity. We share that identity with people from the same culture.

Knowing how this culture has developed helps us understand what life was like in the past. It helps us know where the ideas that are important in our culture today have come from.

Finding out about different places helps us to celebrate different cultures from around the world. We can see how cultures influence each other.

Activity

Draw and write about three aspects of cultural heritage in your country.

1.7 Celebrating local culture

In these lessons you will learn:

- to identify aspects of local culture
- that culture can be creative
- the important parts of the local culture.

Local culture

The effects of culture can be seen everywhere in everyday life. Culture affects the style of buildings in an area. It affects how people behave and what they choose to do with their time. It affects the clothes people choose to wear and the food they choose to eat.

▲ This clothing shows different examples of dress worn in a variety of Islamic cultures.

◀ People meeting and talking in a café is a common sight in Arab cultures.

Celebrating modern culture

Writing books, creating artwork and making craft objects are all ways of celebrating modern culture. Other ways of doing this are through such things as music, drama, dance and film-making.

In many places there are special times and festivals when different parts of culture are celebrated.

Treasuring culture from the past

The culture of the past can be found in old books, and in art and craft objects. Many of these items are displayed in museums today. Some parts of traditional culture are found in music and dance. People learn to play traditional instruments and others learn traditional dances.

Traditional crafts, such as basket-weaving, are also 'kept alive' by people using old craft-making skills.

Remembering and celebrating the past is part of modern culture.

▲ There are many artists working across the Middle East today.

▲ Traditional culture can be kept alive in many ways. These are dancers at a traditional Bedouin wedding celebration in Egypt.

Activities

1 Make a design for an object such as a pot or rug that shows an important part of your culture.

2 Imagine: A box containing eight items (or photographs) that show different parts of your culture today is to be buried in the ground, in the hope that people will find it in a hundred years. Work in a group to choose the items that you think should go in the box.

3 Draw each object that will go into your box and write down why it was chosen.

1.8 Cultures living together

In this lesson you will learn:
- what makes a multicultural society
- how different cultures can be recognised and celebrated.

How cultures begin

People have always lived in groups. When these groups share the same ideas and traditions they make up a society. In the past, the groups did not mix very often. It was not easy to travel long distances. Many people lived their whole lives in the places where they were born. The culture of the groups that made up a society stayed the same.

▲ Many people live in a way that has not changed much for many hundreds of years.

How cultures change

People started to live in cities and began to trade with other places. People from different groups with different cultures started meeting and living in the same place. People were introduced to new ideas from other cultures. The original culture of the place was usually kept as the most important.

Today it is much easier to travel and people often move to live in different parts of the world. When they move they take ideas, beliefs and practices from their culture with them.

◀ It is easy for people today to travel great distances around the world.

Multicultural societies

The term 'multi' simply means *more than one*. So 'multicultural' means more than one culture. In many places today, large groups of people from different countries and cultures are living in the same place. Together they make up one society. Since a number of cultures are mixed together in one society, we say that this is a multicultural society.

In a multicultural society it is important for everyone to respect the ideas, beliefs and behaviour of people from different cultures. However, the ideas and values from the original culture of a place are still the most important. It is the culture that is most likely to affect how people behave and how they dress.

▲ Many people today live in a multicultural society.

Activities

1 Carry out a survey of all the different countries and cultures represented in your class.

2 Make a poster that shows three things from your culture that you think are worth celebrating.

Unit 1 Review questions

1 A person's physical identity is to do with:
   a the way he or she thinks
   b the features of his or her face and body
   c the way he or she feels about things
   d the things he or she is very good at

2 When people have a particular thing they want to achieve, this is often described as:
   a a difficult decision
   b a personal goal
   c a special favour
   d a favourite activity

3 An important thing to learn within a family is:
   a what your favourite food is
   b how to ride a bicycle
   c how to turn on a television
   d to take responsibility for certain chores

4 The parts of culture, including art, music and buildings, that survive from the past are sometimes known as:
   a cultural treasures
   b cultural heritage
   c cultural artefacts
   d cultural monuments

5 In a multicultural society:
   a people from one culture live together
   b there are lots of museums and art galleries
   c people from different cultures live together
   d people enjoy listening to music

6 Write down three things that you would say are important parts of who you are as a person.

7 Write about a special thing you would like to achieve and explain how you will do this.

8 Write about two values that you think have been passed on to you by your family.

9 Describe two examples of cultural heritage that you know of in your country.

10 Describe two values people might need to have if they are living in a multicultural society.

2 History and heritage

In this unit you will learn:

o how evidence helps us learn about the past
o about different sorts of evidence
o about people who lived in our region long ago
o how to look for information on the past
o about the development of trade in the Arabian Peninsula.

? Have you visited any places built a long time ago?

expert

historian

community

nomad

irrigation   peninsula

oral

2.1 Historical evidence

In this lesson you will learn:
- about how we find out about the past.

If we want to find out about the past we need evidence.

Evidence for the recent past

We can get some information about the recent past from older people who remember what it was like in the earlier part of their life. We call this **oral** evidence.

▲ People who are older can remember life in their past.

We can also find things that were written during this time and we can look at objects and art.

Evidence from the distant past

As we go further back in time we only have writings, art and objects to help us know what life was like. There are no people left alive from those times to tell us.

Many different kinds of writing are useful. The documents kept by important people and the letters ordinary people wrote to each other can all give us **clues** about life in their time.

Official documents might tell us about all the things owned by a king or another kind of ruler.

Sometimes there is no writing and we just find objects. **Experts** work out what the objects were and how they may have been used. We then decide what the object tells us about life in the time from which it comes.

▲ Very old writings are in languages that we do not use today.

Works of art give us many clues about life in different times. We can see what people are wearing. Sometimes we can see the kinds of houses they lived in, the transport they used and the instruments they played.

◀ Old paintings and drawings can show us some parts of what life was like in the past, such as the clothes people wore.

▲ Objects can tell us things about the past. What do you think this object is? Who may have owned it?

Activities

1 Work in a group to make a list of things you think your parents or grandparents would be able to tell you about life in the recent past.

2 Draw an object from today that you think would be in a museum in the future. Write about what the object would tell people about life today.

2.2 Evidence for local history

In this lesson you will learn:
○ about the different types of evidence that gives information about important events in local history.

Historians want to know what life was like in the past. They want to know what people did, how they lived, and how they organised themselves.

? What sort of evidence might be found in countries of the Arabian Gulf?

Evidence from buildings

People who lived as hunter-gatherers were always moving. They have left no evidence in the form of buildings because they lived in caves or built shelters from rocks, branches and animal skin.

Once people began to settle in one place they built villages and towns. They used mud bricks that lasted a long time. Some of these old places were abandoned. Sometimes people stayed in the old towns or cities and built more houses as more people arrived to live there. Some old structures are still in use today.

◀ Old buildings can tell us a lot about how people lived. These are wind towers in Dubai.

Evidence from objects

The early hunter-gatherers made things like spearheads and arrowheads from stone. By the time people became farmers they had also invented pottery. This allowed them to make jars in which they could store food and liquids.

Different materials such as metals were discovered. Techniques for making new metals and for creating glass developed. Objects were made from these new materials.

▲ These pieces of pottery found in Egypt show us that early populations had skilled craftsmen and women.

Evidence from writing and art

When writing was invented it was used to record both major events and small happenings in everyday life. People have used art to record what they see for thousands of years.

▲ Objects are found buried in the ground at different depths. Older objects are usually found at deeper levels.

Activities

1 In a group, discuss what the items in the different layers shown in the picture on the left tell us about different times.

2 Work in a group to find out about an old building in your area. Find out how old it is, what it was originally used for, and what it is used for now.

2.3 Early history

In this lesson you will learn:
- about the people who lived a very long time ago
- about how people settled in different parts of the Arabian Peninsula.

Hunter-gatherers

A very long time ago, before people settled permanently in particular places, they moved around and got the food they needed from hunting wild animals and from collecting food from plants and trees. They were known as hunter-gatherers.

This was a time before writing had been invented and so nothing was written down. We know about them only because of some evidence we find, such as pieces of pottery or arrowheads. Sometimes we find images they drew which show people hunting or gathered around a fire.

▲ This type of ancient painting is sometimes found in caves and tells us about the life of people who lived long ago.

Farmers and fishermen

Hunter-gatherers relied on the land to provide plants and wild animals for food. If the area where they lived did not have these then they needed to move. At a certain time in the past the climate in the Arabian **Peninsula** changed and became hot and dry. Rivers that had once flowed dried up and the area was covered in **scrublands** and deserts.

There were not enough animals or plants here and so the people who lived there at that time moved to the mountains, valleys, oases and to the coast. Here they became farmers and fishermen. The farmers grew crops like wheat, rice and millet. Some farmers raised animals too. They were able to stay in the same place and so villages and towns grew up.

Some of the people preferred to take their animals from place to place looking for food and water. People who do this are called **nomads**. This lifestyle is an important and noble tradition in the Arabian Peninsula.

▲ These are the remains of an early settlement in Al Hajir, Jebel Shams, Al Hajar Mountains, Oman.

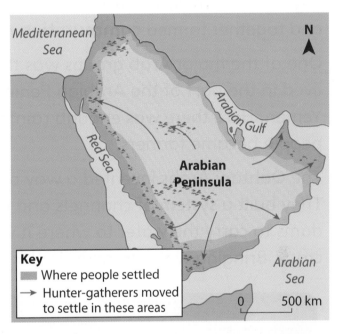

▲ This map shows areas where people settled when they were no longer hunter-gatherers.

Activities

1 Work in a group to discuss the different foods that would be available for the different groups of people who became settled farmers, fishermen and nomadic herders.

2 Look at the map and decide what conditions may have been like in the places people moved to.

2.4 Early tribes and trade

In this lesson you will learn:
- about the early tribes who lived in the Arabian Peninsula
- about how trade developed.

Early tribes

There is a long tradition of peoples in the Arabian Peninsula living together in **tribes**. This means that they lived in their family groups and together formed **communities** which shared the same culture.

One of the major Arab groups was the Qahtani. The Qahtani lived in the part of the Arabian Peninsula that we now know as Yemen. Here there was enough rainfall to grow crops and the people became farmers.

The Qahtani Arabs invented a way of storing water in **dams**. They built a system of channels and tunnels leading from the dams to carry the water to where it was needed to water the crops. Bringing water to crops in this way is known as **irrigation**.

▲ One of the largest of the ancient dams was Ma'rib Dam, which was first built almost 4000 years ago.

Many Qahtani tribes decided to leave this area when the land could not provide for all their needs. They spread throughout the Arabian Peninsula and beyond.

Another large Arab group was the Adnanites. These people lived in northern, central and western Arabia.

Trade

People in ancient times in Arabia became traders and merchants. When people trade, they exchange goods between them.

Trade became very important and goods were exchanged with many other countries in different parts of the world.

Lots of people wanted the things that came from the Arabian Peninsula, such as dates and spices. Some of the most precious goods were types of **incense** which were found in the areas now known as Yemen and Oman.

Trade by boat meant that ports on the coasts became very important. Trade across land created many routes for people to travel along.

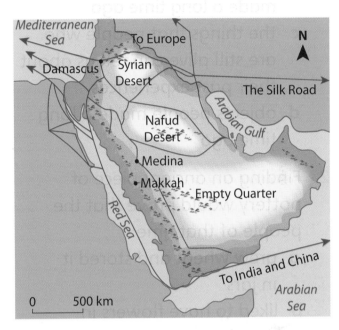

▲ This map shows old routes used by traders in the Arabian Peninsula.

▲ Dates have been an important part of trade for many hundreds of years.

Activities

1 Find out about some of the things traded by people in ancient times. Draw and label three items.

2 Draw a timeline to show how the things people did in the Arabian Peninsula changed over time.

Unit 2 Review questions

1 Oral evidence about the past is:
   a written documents that people wrote a long time ago
   b drawings and paintings people made a long time ago
   c the things that people who are still alive can tell us about their past experiences
   d objects people made a long time ago

2 Finding an ancient piece of pottery would prove that the people of that time:
   a grew wheat and stored it in jars
   b liked to have flowers in their homes
   c carried water in jars on their heads
   d had the resources, knowledge and skills to make pottery

3 Objects we find in the ground can tell us about the past. Older objects are usually found:
   a near the surface
   b deeper underground
   c near water
   d near trees

4 People who herd animals from place to place in search of food and water are known as:
   a nomads
   b wanderers
   c settlers
   d farmers

5 The written records of an ancient trader would reveal that people of the time could write. Write two other things that the records might reveal.

6 Write three things that the ruins of an old building or settlement might tell us about life in the past.

7 Give two possible reasons for people in the past choosing to settle on the coasts of the Arabian Peninsula.

8 Write about two items that have been an important part of trade in the Arabian Peninsula.

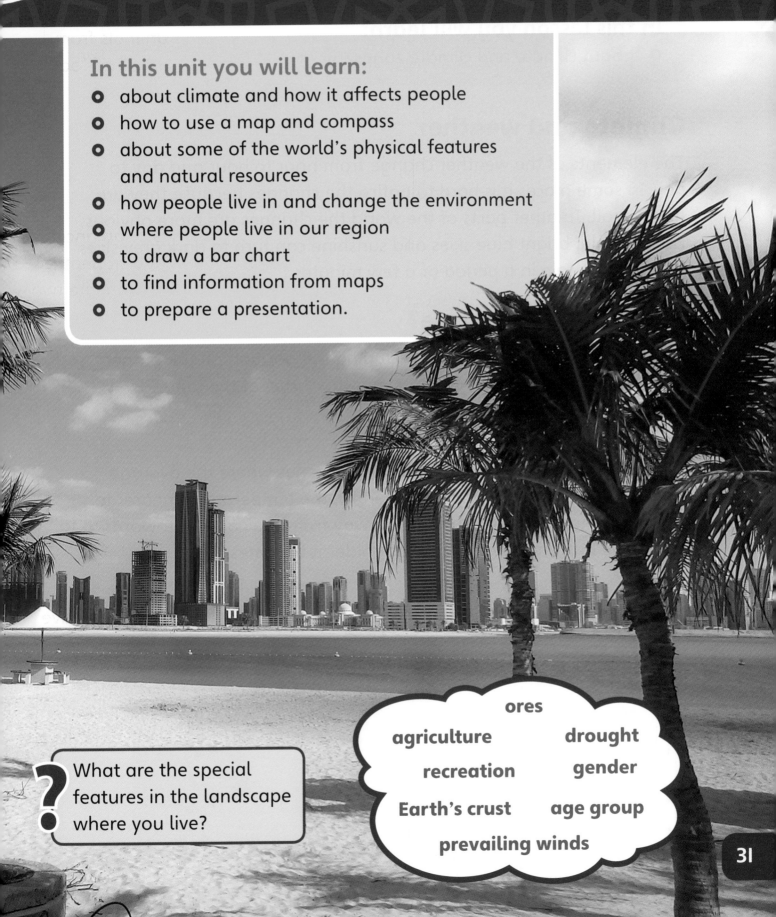

3 People and places

In this unit you will learn:
- about climate and how it affects people
- how to use a map and compass
- about some of the world's physical features and natural resources
- how people live in and change the environment
- where people live in our region
- to draw a bar chart
- to find information from maps
- to prepare a presentation.

? What are the special features in the landscape where you live?

ores
agriculture   drought
recreation   gender
Earth's crust   age group
prevailing winds

3.1 Climate

In this lesson you will learn:
- about climate and climate zones.

Climate and weather

The elements of the weather change from hour to hour and day to day. In some places it is hard to notice the changes because they are quite small. In other parts of the world the changes are more obvious. For example, bright blue skies and sunshine can turn to dark grey skies and pouring rain in a period of a few minutes.

What affects climate?

Many things affect the climate, including the position on the planet, **prevailing winds**, ocean currents and the shape of the land.

Climate zones

Scientists divide the world up into climate zones where the average weather conditions are similar. Generally, the temperatures nearer to the equator are higher. The further away from the equator towards the top or bottom of the Earth, the colder it becomes.

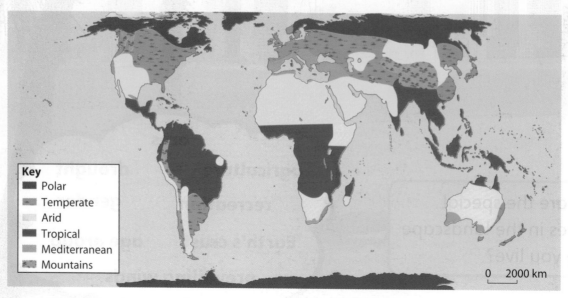

Key
- Polar
- Temperate
- Arid
- Tropical
- Mediterranean
- Mountains

0   2000 km

▲ The world's climate zones.

Temperatures in the polar climate are very low. There are strong winds and heavy snows.

Temperate climates do not have extremes of high or low temperatures. Rain falls throughout the year.

Arid climate zones have very little rain and very high temperatures.

Tropical climates have warm temperatures and only two seasons: a 'wet season' of heavy rains and a 'dry season' where little or no rain falls at all.

◀ Heavy rain in the rainy season in the tropical zone can lead to flooding.

A Mediterranean climate has warm to hot summers and mild winters. There is little rain and very little snow except on the mountains.

Very high mountains around the world have their own climate where it is always cold and the ground is permanently covered with snow.

▲ People cannot live in the high areas of the mountain climate zone.

Activities

1 Choose a climate zone and then use maps or atlases to find a particular town and country within that zone.

2 Write a list of all you would need to take with you if you visited that place.

3.2 Climate and human activity

In this lesson you will learn:
- how human activity is affected by climate and weather.

Climate zones and human activity

Each of the climate zones on Earth presents different challenges for people.

Living is very difficult in the climate zones with extremes of temperature, whether that is very cold or very hot. No people live permanently in the coldest parts of the polar climate zone because they cannot survive in the freezing temperatures and there is not enough food. In the warmer parts of the polar zone, people have traditionally lived a nomadic life, herding reindeer.

◄ Much of the polar climate zone is permanently covered with snow and ice.

The very high temperatures of the arid zone make it difficult for people to survive here. The ground does not receive enough rainfall to allow many plants to **germinate**, so few food crops can be grown, and there is a limited supply of drinking water. In countries in the arid zone, human activity is usually concentrated around sources of water.

Tropical zones are usually able to support the growth of food plants over wider areas. Problems arise here because the year is divided into a rainy season and a dry season. If there is a long dry season with little or no rain, this is called a **drought**.

▲ In a drought, seeds find it difficult to grow, and crops that are already growing will wither and die.

The temperate and Mediterranean climate zones do not have the extremes of temperature of the polar and arid zones. Here too there are more gradual changes in the amount of rainfall compared with the distinct wet and dry seasons of the tropics. These climate zones therefore offer a wide range of opportunities for human activity and permanent settlement.

◄ Areas of grassland in the temperate zone provide food for grazing animals like sheep and cattle.

Activity

Make a fact sheet about the Earth's climate zones. Your sheet should explain briefly what the climate is like in each zone, and how these climate conditions affect people's lives.

In this lesson you will learn:

- about a compass and a compass rose
- about the eight compass points
- to use the eight compass points to describe position on a map.

▲ We use a compass to find out directions.

A compass

A compass is a special instrument. It has a face a bit like a watch. Instead of numbers around the face, a compass has different directions. The main directions, working 'clockwise', are north, east, south and west.

The directions in-between these points are made by joining the two main directions together. So the direction between north and west is north-west. The direction between south and east is south-east.

The compass also has a pointer inside called a 'needle'. This needle points in the direction of north.

To read the compass you move it around until the north shown on the face lines up with the direction in which the needle is pointing. You can then read off all the other directions.

A compass rose

A compass rose is a design on a map that shows direction.

A compass rose is often placed so that North points to the top of the map. However, most maps include only a simple North point to show direction, not a complete 'rose' – see the map on the next page.

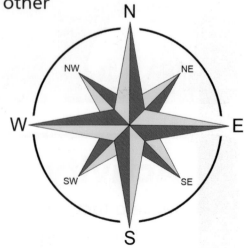

▲ This compass rose shows eight directions.

Directions on a map

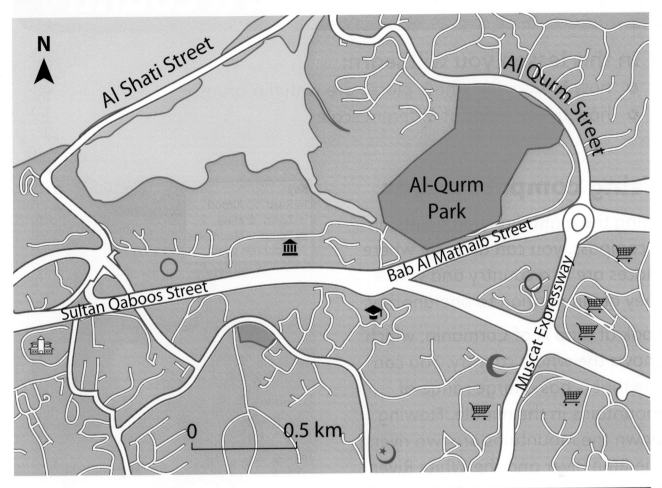

▲ This map shows a part of Muscat.

Key
- 🟦 Park
- 🏛 Museum
- ☽ Mosque
- 🏫 School
- 🎓 College
- ◯ Police station
- ☾ Hospital
- ◯ Hotel
- 🛒 Shops

Activities

1 Using the map above, answer these questions:

- In which direction is the school from the small park?

- What do you find if you travel south from the college?

- What is north-east of the hospital?

2 Work with a partner and describe the directions you need to travel to get from one place to another on the map.

In this lesson you will learn:

- how to describe where places are within a country
- how to use maps at different scales.

Using compass points

Using the eight direction points on a compass, you can describe where places are in a country and where they are in relation to one another.

Look at map A of Carmania, which shows the whole country. You can see that is has a large range of mountains in the middle. Flowing down the mountains are two rivers, the Blue River and the White River. Most people live in the towns: Main Town, Big Town and Small Town. Tourists to the country like to visit Moffat's Cave, and the beaches in the bays are very popular with everybody in the summer.

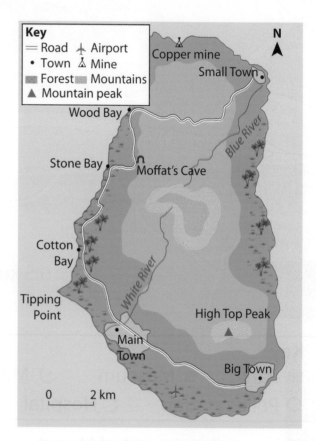

▲ **A** A map of the imaginary country of Carmania.

Scale on a map

Maps cannot show things at the size they are in real life, so they are drawn to scale. Maps show things smaller than in real life. Each measurement on a map stands for a different measurement in real life.

Looking at maps of different scales is like 'zooming in' and 'zooming out'.

When you 'zoom in' you can see more detail but you cannot see such a large area.

When you 'zoom out' you can see a larger area but not so much detail.

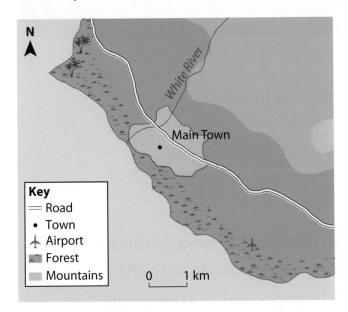

Key
= Road
• Town
✈ Airport
▦ Forest
▨ Mountains
0   1 km

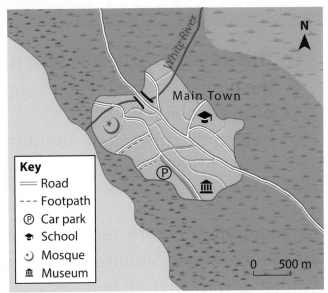

Key
= Road
--- Footpath
Ⓟ Car park
🏫 School
☾ Mosque
🏛 Museum
0   500 m

▲ B The scale on this map shows that for every I cm on the map there is I km on the ground. The map shows more detail than map A.

▲ C The scale on this map shows that for every I cm on the map there is 0.5 km on the ground. It shows even more detail than map B.

Activities

1 Use map A of Carmania to answer these questions.

- Small Town is in the north-east part of Carmania. In which part of the country is Big Town?

- If you take the road from Wood Bay towards Small Town, in which direction are you travelling?

- The White River flows down the mountains towards Main Town. In which direction does it flow?

- If you take the road from Moffat's Cave towards Wood Bay, in which direction are you travelling?

- Which bay is furthest west?

2 Work with a partner. Make up some direction and location questions about the map to ask each other.

3 Write down two things that you can see on map C that are not on map A.

3.5 Regions

In this lesson you will learn:

- the names of countries and capital cities in the region of the Arabian Gulf
- how to describe where countries are within the region of the Arabian Gulf.

In geography, the word 'region' is used to describe an area of land that has some common features. These features may be to do with the climate, or with physical features such as high ground or coastal plains.

The size of a region can vary a great deal. If we refer to the 'coastal region' of a country we mean only the part of a country near the coast. A larger region can include several countries.

The region of the Middle East

The Middle East is in an important position for trade between different countries.

The Arabian Peninsula

Within the region known as the Middle East is the region of the Arabian Peninsula. This is the area of land that is bounded on the west by the Red Sea, on the north-east by the Arabian Gulf, and by the Arabian Sea and Indian Ocean to the south-east.

There are seven countries within the Arabian Peninsula: Saudi Arabia, Kuwait, Bahrain, Qatar, UAE, Oman and Yemen. These are often referred to as a region. All except Yemen form the Arabian Gulf region as they have coastlines along the Arabian Gulf.

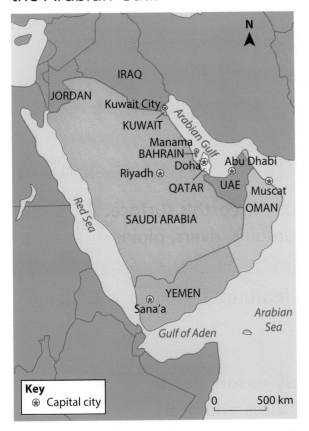

▲ A Countries of the Arabian Peninsula, showing capital cities.

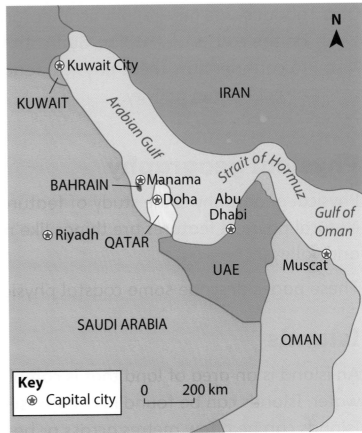

▲ B Countries of the Arabian Gulf.

Activities

Answer these questions.

Map A

1 Which is the largest country in the Arabian Peninsula?

2 Which country has a coast on the Arabian Sea and the Red Sea?

Map B

3 Name the capital cities of Qatar and Bahrain.

4 Which country has borders with the United Arab Emirates, Saudi Arabia and Yemen?

3.6 Natural coastal features

In this lesson you will learn:
- about some natural physical features found on the coasts of Arabian Gulf countries
- to consider how these physical features affect human activity.

Physical geography

Physical geography is the study of features of the Earth's surface. Natural physical features are things like mountains, rivers, plains and valleys.

These pages describe some coastal physical features.

Islands

An island is an area of land that is completely surrounded by water. Islands can be found in oceans, seas, lakes and rivers. Islands can be a few metres across or be large enough to be a country, such as Bahrain.

◀ There are many islands off the coast of Abu Dhabi.

Inlets

An inlet is a feature where water leads off from its main 'body' to form a narrow 'arm'. An inlet on the seashore leads inland. An inlet from a river leads into the land beyond the river bank.

Inlets from the sea are useful because they can provide a natural harbour for ships. This gives them protection from the conditions on the open sea. A creek is one form of an inlet.

Bays and coves

A bay is a type of inlet where quite a large body of water curves inland. If the land curves round and encloses the body of water, giving more shelter, this is known as a cove.

Salt marshes

A salt marsh is an area of low ground near the coast that is always wet with sea water or is often flooded by the sea. These areas are habitats for special plants and animals.

Beaches

A beach is a sloping area of sand or pebbles on a shoreline. It is the area covered by the sea between low tide and high tide. Many beaches in countries of the Arabian Gulf have a gentle slope and fine sand. This makes them very attractive and popular with visitors.

▲ Dubai Creek.

▲ Salt marshes, like these in South Africa, are found in many coastal areas of the Arabian Gulf.

▲ A beach in Dubai.

Activity

Work in a group to find out about some coastal features in your country. Describe how these features are used by people.

3.7 Inland physical features

In this lesson you will learn:
- about some natural physical features found inland in Arabian Gulf countries
- to consider how these physical features affect human activity.

Deserts

A desert is a large, often sandy area where there is very little rain. Very few plants can grow in these conditions and so there is little or no vegetation. The lack of water and the difficulty with growing food makes it hard for people to live in a desert.

Much of the central area of the Arabian Peninsula is desert, known as the 'Empty Quarter'. This extends into the countries of the Arabian Gulf. Most human settlement takes place along the coasts.

◀ Desert regions are dry and hardly anything grows.

Did you know?
The Rub' al Khali or 'Empty Quarter' is the biggest sand desert in the world. It covers large parts of Saudi Arabia, Yemen, Oman and the United Arab Emirates.

Mountains

A mountain is an area of the Earth's surface where the land rises steeply and to a great height. The highest point of a mountain is called the summit. When the summit is pointed and narrow it is called a peak. Several mountains together in one area form a 'mountain range' or 'mountain chain'.

The Hajar Mountains are in the east of the United Arab Emirates and north-eastern Oman. The climate in the Hajar Mountains is cool and wet from December to March and there is occasional rain at other times. This means more plants and trees grow. This helps animals to survive.

▲ Mountain areas of the Arabian Gulf have more rain than the low land.

Plains

A plain is an area of flat land. In Arabian Gulf countries there are stony desert plains and also plains along the coasts. Plains can be very useful for growing crops as the soil there is often very **fertile**.

Al-Batinah is a coastal plain in north-east Oman. The Jiri Plain in the northern Emirates separates the mountains in the east from the desert in the west.

▲ These fertile coastal plains are places where food crop and animal farming take place.

Plateaus

A plateau is a high-level plain.

▲ The Jiddat-al-Harasis plateau in Oman.

Activities

1 Work in a group to prepare a presentation about an inland physical feature in your country.

2 Write a short explanation of why it would be harder to live in a desert than on a coastal plain.

In this lesson you will learn:
- about some natural physical features connected with water
- to consider how these physical features affect human activity.

Valleys

A valley is a long area of low land between mountains or hills. A valley often has a river or stream running along the bottom. The water in the valley may dry up during times of little or no rainfall. The term *wadi* is usually given to those valleys that are dry except during the rainy season. Wadis are found in countries in the Arabian Gulf where there are no permanent rivers.

◀ A dry wadi.

◀ A flooded wadi.

Oases

An oasis is an area in the desert where water can be found. The water comes from under the ground. The water might be in the form of a stream that flows underground. Water is also sometimes stored in the rocks themselves, which act like a sponge. The water travels through the rock and where it comes to the surface there is an oasis.

Oases have always been important for nomadic people living in the desert and for those travelling through as merchants. Oases became places where permanent settlements grew. They were important centres of **agriculture** and that is still true today.

◀ The village of Balad Seet in Oman.

> **Did you know?**
> The oasis at Al Ain in Abu Dhabi emirate has been the site of a permanent settlement for 5,000 years.

Caves

A cave is a passage or hollow under the ground that has been formed by natural processes. The force of the water slowly wears some of the rock away to form the cave. Caves found inland are usually formed by water slowly dissolving the rock. Sea caves are found on the coast where they are formed by the waves hitting a **cliff** face.

Caves have been used by people as shelter for thousands of years. Today caves can be popular tourist attractions.

▲ Caves are very special natural features.

Activities

1 Work in a group to find out about some natural features associated with water in your country.

2 Draw and write about one of the features you found out about in Activity 1 and explain how it is used today.

3.9 Mapping physical features

In this lesson you will learn:

○ how physical features are shown on maps.

Natural physical features on maps

Maps that show the height and depth of physical features such as mountains and valleys are called relief maps. Like all maps they can be drawn at different scales.

It is useful to know the different heights of areas of land because this can have an effect on rainfall, and on how easy it is to travel.

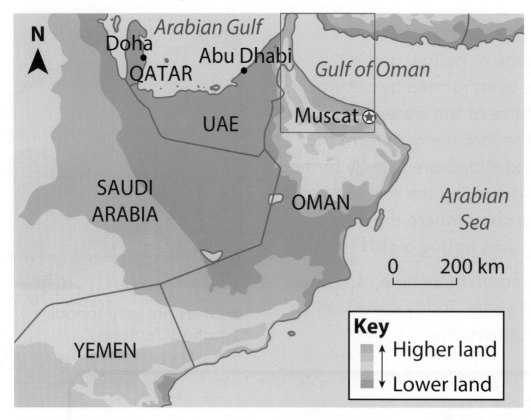

▲ **A** This map shows the height of land in different places. It covers a wide area and does not give much detail.

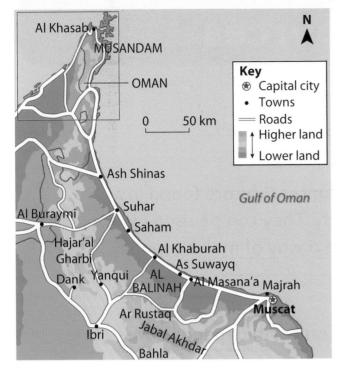

▲ **B** This map shows the area in the rectangle on map A at a larger scale.

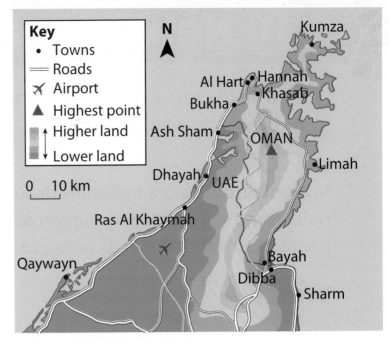

▲ **C** This is the area of the rectangle in map B.

Map B shows a section of the north coast of Oman and the United Arab Emirates. It gives more detail, including the position of some towns and roads.

A map with more detail, as in map C, lets you see even more clearly the shape of the coast and the location of lakes and rivers. You can also see areas of high ground and mountains. The highest point on the map is marked with a special symbol.

Activities

Work with a partner.

1 Describe how the landscape in Oman is different from the landscape in the United Arab Emirates.

2 Looking at maps B and C, can you think why the main roads are near the coast?

3 An airport is shown on map C. Describe what you think the landscape there is like.

3.10 Natural resources

In this lesson you will learn:
- about some natural resources.

Natural resources are materials or substances that are found in nature and not created by human activity. They can be used by people to meet their needs or to provide a way of making money.

Water

Water is a vital natural resource. All life on Earth depends on it for survival.

People drink water and use it for many other purposes in the home and in farming. Water is also used in many other kinds of industry.

Land

Land is another very important natural resource. People live on land and they use it in different ways. We say there are 'competing' land uses because there is a need for many types of use. For example, we need to use some land to build houses on because people need places to live. We also need to use some land to grow food and keep animals to provide for our food needs.

Trees

Trees grow naturally and create forests. Trees supply wood and timber products and also many other useful resources including food and the **ingredients** for some medicines.

▲ Many useful items can be made from trees and their wood.

Fish and seafood

Fish and other sea creatures live naturally in the oceans.
People take mostly fish from the natural stock in the sea.

▲ The world's seas provide food for millions of people.

Minerals and metals

Minerals are naturally occurring, non-living solid substances,
for example different types of rock. Some rocks, called **ores**,
contain material from which we get metals.

▲ Copper is a metal that is used to make many items including
wire for electrical items, pipes and eating and cooking utensils.

Oil and gas

Oil and gas are both found
buried deep in the **Earth's
crust**. These are used in many
different ways but are most
important as sources of fuel.

Activity

Draw and write about how
each of the natural resources
named on these pages is used.

3.11 The Arabian Gulf

In this lesson you will learn:
○ about natural resources found in the Arabian Gulf.

Land and water

Land and water are very valuable resources in Arabian Gulf countries. Some land is used for building towns and cities. Some land must also be used to provide food. Water is needed for people to drink but it is also vital for agriculture.

◄ The dam at Wadi Dayqah is the largest in Oman. The water is used by villagers and for agriculture.

Much of the water used by people in the region comes from the sea. The salt must be taken out of it first. This process is called **desalination**.

Trees

Most of the trees grown in Arabian Gulf countries are for food, such as dates and citrus fruits, rather than for timber. Another important product is frankincense. It is made from the **resin** of certain trees which grow in Oman and Yemen. It is valuable because of its lovely smell and has been traded around the world for thousands of years. Mangroves grow in the salt marshes found in some places on the coast and they make important animal habitats.

▲ Dates have been an important food resource in the region for thousands of years.

Fish and seafood

Fish are caught in the Arabian Gulf, in the Gulf of Oman and the waters of the Arabian Sea. Favourite local fish are hamour and kingfish. Most of the fish is eaten in the country where it is landed, and a lot more is brought in from other countries.

Minerals and metals

Many mineral rocks found in the Arabian Gulf are useful for such things as making roads and building houses. Some mines produce copper and other metals including **chromium**.

▲ Chromium is a metal. It is used to make stainless steel which is often used to make cutlery. A thin layer of chromium is sometimes put around objects to make them look shiny. This is called chrome plating.

Oil and gas

Oil and gas are the two resources that have brought most wealth to the countries of the region. Most of the oil and gas from this region is sold to other countries around the world.

Activities

1. Make a list of the natural resources described on these pages. Write about some way in which you have used each one.

2. Make a class display of things that are made in your country using local resources.

3.12 Changing the environment

In these lessons you will learn:
- how human activity changes the environment
- about physical features built by people in Arabian Gulf countries.

When early people settled in an area they had to make changes to the natural environment. In some places they needed to clear the natural vegetation. On the cleared land they built houses, planted crops or kept animals.

They did these things to meet their basic needs.

We still change the environment to meet our needs today.

Settlements

Most people today live in towns and cities where all they need is provided. There are different areas where people live, work and shop. There are also places for education, places of worship, and public parks where people can relax in beautiful surroundings.

▲ The central area of a modern town has tower blocks containing offices, hotels and apartments.

Food

Food is grown away from the large towns and cities. Land is watered so that crops will grow. Crops are sometimes grown in special buildings called greenhouses.

Food is brought in to the city. A lot of our food today is transported in planes and ships around the world.

▲ The natural environment is changed so that people can grow food.

Industry

We change the environment to obtain resources from mines and quarries. We build things for other **industries** including factories for **manufacturing**, offices for business and oil wells, refineries and power stations for energy.

Transport

We build modern transport systems to move people around and between towns and cities. People and goods are also transported over larger distances, using planes and ships. We build airports for planes and seaports for ships to load and unload passengers and **cargo**.

▲ Large ships carry goods all around the world.

Activities

1 Write about three physical features in your locality that were built by people.

2 Work in a group to design a plan for a modern settlement. Your plan should show areas that together provide for all the needs of the people who live there.

3.13 Transport

In this lesson you will learn:
- about different types of transport
- why different forms of transport are used.

Land transport

People and goods travel over land in different types of transport.

Private transport is transport that is owned or used by private individuals or companies. Cars are the most common form of private transport. People use these to move around, especially over shorter distances.

Private companies use trucks of different shapes and sizes to move goods.

Public transport is transport that is used by members of the public. Types of public transport in cities include taxis, buses, trams, monorail and metrorail.

◄ Buses carry people around towns and cities and link with other forms of transport.

Water transport

Some people have private boats. These are most often used for pleasure and **recreation**.

Examples of local public transport across water are ferries and water taxis. Water taxis, called *abras*, are small boats that travel short distances. Larger boats are used for longer journeys.

Large boats are also used to carry raw materials and other goods around the world. Large ships use specially built **docks** in a port.

◀ Fishing vessels and boats that carry tourists are a common sight in the waters of the Arabian Gulf and the Gulf of Oman.

Air transport

People, packages and goods are all transported over longer distances by air. Some people and companies have private planes or helicopters.

Countries have international airports where planes can take off and land. These airports are usually built away from towns and cities. There are transport links so that people can get from the airport to where they need to go.

Walking and cycling

Health experts want more people to be active. A good way to be active is to walk or cycle whenever possible and where it is safe to do so.

▲ The region's modern cities have special areas designed for safe walking and cycling, as here in Abu Dhabi.

Activities

1 Draw and write about the different types of transport you can see in your local area.

2 Write about some places you know where people can walk and cycle.

3.14 Populations

Population

A population is all the people who live in any given area, such as a village, a town or a country.

Knowing about the population helps to match the needs of the population with the resources available to meet those needs.

▲ Many people around the world live in cities.

The characteristics of a population are to do with the similarities and differences between the people, such as their ages and **gender**. It is important to know this because different people have different needs.

Age

Populations are made up of people from different **age groups** who need different things. For example, children need places to go to school and adults need places to work. The mix of age groups can change over time.

▲ Many young children go to kindergarten.

Gender

Populations are made up of groups of men and women, boys and girls.

Culture

Many populations today are made up of people who come from different countries. These people bring their own culture, ideas and beliefs.

◀ City populations have people from countries around the world.

Changing populations

Populations are always changing. People grow older and new babies are born. People move into an area to work and others move away.

Activities

1 Make a bar chart that shows information about the population of your class.

- How many pupils are in the class altogether?

- How many pupils are boys and how many are girls?

- If every person in the class uses three pencils and two pens in a year, how many pens and pencils must the school provide?

2 Draw and write about what different people in a population need.

In these lessons you will learn:
- why people choose to live in certain places.

Where people lived in the past

In the past, people chose the places where they would make settlements for a number of reasons. They thought about the things they would need to survive. They also had to think about the resources they would need if they were going to build a settlement. They might think about how they would keep themselves safe.

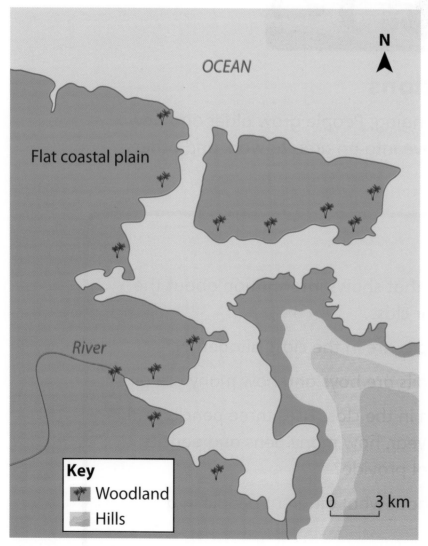

N

OCEAN

Flat coastal plain

River

Key
- Woodland
- Hills

0   3 km

▲ **A** This map shows a small section of a coastal area.

Where people live today

People today choose where they will live for different reasons. They still need to know that they will be able to get all the things they need to survive and to live an enjoyable life. How they get these things is different from people in the past. The range of needs and wants that people have has changed over time.

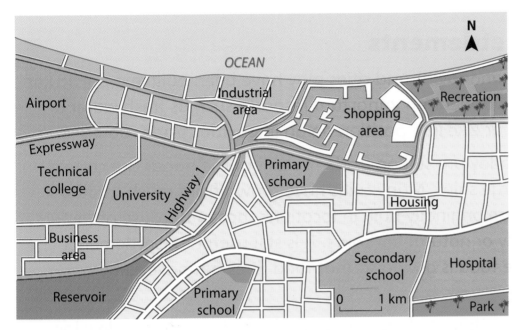

▲ **B** This map shows a small section of a modern coastal town.

Activities

1 Work in a group. Decide why people in the past may have chosen to build a settlement in the area shown in map A.

2 On a large copy of map A, mark where you think *you* would build a settlement. Then label other parts of your map to show the sorts of activities that people might have carried out there.

3 Still working in a group, decide why people might choose to live in the area shown in map B.

4 Make a list of some of the reasons for your decision. Explain how these are different from the reasons people in the past had for choosing where to live.

In this lesson you will learn:

○ about the main settlements in countries of the Arabian Gulf.

Location of settlements

In the past, villages and towns and cities may have been built in a particular location because it was near an important resource such as fresh water or good farming land, or else in a position on an important trade route.

Some settlements today are still on trade routes but the goods are carried by aeroplanes or large ships. Many cities have grown from much smaller settlements that were originally built in locations chosen because of factors such as water supply or natural harbours. It is still useful for settlements to be close to where food is grown so that food does not have to be transported too far.

In countries on the Arabian Gulf, the area where settlements can develop is also affected by the extent of the desert.

Activities

Refer to the maps on the next page to help you answer these questions:

1 Make a list of the countries and capital cities in the Arabian Gulf region.

2 What do you notice about the location of all the capital cities apart from Riyadh?

3 Write why you think most people in these countries live in cities.

4 What might you find at cities located inland?

5 Write about the transport links you think these places have with other countries around the world.

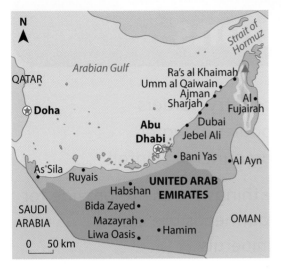

▲ United Arab Emirates and its main cities.

Key to all maps
- ✪ Capital city
- • Main towns
- ✈ Airport
- ▲ Highest point
- Higher land
- Lower land

▲ Qatar and its main cities.

▲ Oman and its main cities.

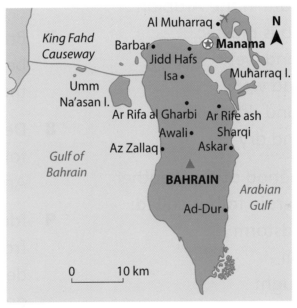

▲ Bahrain and its main cities.

▲ Kuwait and its main cities.

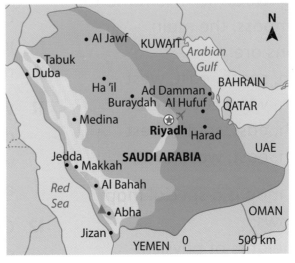

▲ Saudi Arabia and its main cities.

3 People and places

63

Unit 3 Review questions

1 The climate in a place is:
   a the different weather every day
   b the average weather conditions over a long period of time
   c the type of landscape
   d the level of pollution

2 The climate in the Arabian Peninsula is mostly:
   a cold and wet
   b hot and wet
   c cool and dry
   d hot and dry

3 A long period of dry weather when no rain falls is called:
   a a sandstorm
   b a wadi
   c a drought
   d a downpour

4 Reading 'clockwise' from the top of a compass, the main directions are:
   a north, south, east, west
   b north, west, south, east
   c north, east, south, west
   d north, east, west, south

5 A relief map is a special map that shows:
   a the heights of physical features

   b country borders
   c bodies of water
   d amounts of rainfall

6 The things we use to provide for all our needs are called:
   a minerals
   b raw materials
   c resources
   d energy

7 Briefly describe the differences between maps of the same area that are drawn to different scales.

8 Describe two natural features found along the coasts of the Arabian Peninsula.

9 Identify two natural resources from your region and briefly describe ways in which they are used.

10 Describe how two activities carried out by people make important changes to the natural environment.

11 Write about some of the differences between the people who make up the population of a country.

12 Give three reasons why people might choose to live in a modern city.

4 Citizenship

In this unit you will learn:

- what it means to be part of society
- how to use resources carefully
- the ways in which people communicate
- why people need to work
- about the choices people make
- how to conduct a survey
- to design a poster, and write letters and leaflets.

? Why might people be encouraged to use public transport?

policies   durable

disposable   raw materials

consumable   re-usable

ethics

4.1 Being a part of society

In these lessons you will learn:
- about what it means to be a citizen
- how good citizens behave
- the benefits of positive behaviour for society.

What is a society?

A society is made up of people who live together in organised communities and who share similar traditions, values and ideas. A society also has a set of rules or laws that everyone is expected to obey.

▲ A society is made up of all the people who live in a particular area.

All of these things help the people in a society to live together. If they share and respect traditions, this helps them to understand one another. If they have the same values then they are more able to respect each other and treat each other well. If they share ideas about how they want the society to be, then they can all work together to make that happen.

◄ Simply showing good manners can help to create a happier society.

A country's laws should make sure that everyone can be treated fairly. Everyone knows the things they should do and the things they should not do.

Being part of a society

Being part of a society is like being part of a big group. We get some benefits from belonging to a group but we also have responsibilities.

A good member of a society behaves in a way that the society expects. He or she also cares about the feelings and rights of other people. He or she is concerned about other people's safety and wellbeing.

Good members of a society are aware of things that are happening around them. They want to make good use of the society's resources.

They want to be involved and use their skills in making a better society for everyone.

▲ Many people take part in events to help improve their local environment. These people are taking part in a beach clean-up.

Activities

1 Work in a group to discuss the values, ideas and rules in your school. Make a poster that explains how these help in the life of the school.

2 Make a list of the ways in which you could get involved in the school community to help make it a better place.

4.2 A multicultural society

In this lesson you will learn:
- what a multicultural society is
- rights and responsibilities in a multicultural society.

Populations in the past

Earlier populations of Arabian Gulf countries shared the same culture, based on a common Arab heritage and the faith of Islam. The culture and lifestyle did not change for a very long time.

◄ People in the past worked in traditional roles and shared the same ideas.

The modern era

The development of the oil industries in the 1960s brought about big changes. Many people from India and Pakistan came to live and work in the Arabian Gulf. Since then the region has become important for **global** business and people from many different countries are moving here.

Multicultural society

A person's culture is an important part of their identity. All the people coming to live in the countries of the Arabian Gulf bring something of their own culture.

The result of this is that societies in Arabian Gulf countries are multicultural.

▲ Today, people living in the same place often have different cultures.

Responsibilities in a multicultural society

In a multicultural society it is important to respect and value different cultures. People should not do anything to upset or **offend** people from a culture that is different to their own.

Some ideas and values are important in almost all cultures. People value kindness and honesty. They show respect and they hope to be respected in return. Most people like the idea of being able to live in peace with others.

▲ In countries of the Arabian Gulf, traditional Arab and Islamic cultures affect how people live, dress and behave.

Did you know?

Showing the sole of your shoe to someone is considered a sign of disrespect in Arab cultures.

Activity

Make a labelled drawing. In the centre show some of the ideas and values that people have in common. Around this show some of the differences, such as clothing or food, which are special to some of the cultures represented in your school or community.

4.3 Using natural resources

In these lessons you will learn:
- why it is important to use resources carefully
- how using resources carefully is part of being a good citizen.

Shared resources in school

Items that last a long time are described as being **durable**. Items that are used up are **consumable**.

Whether an item is durable or consumable, it should be used correctly and carefully. If a durable item is misused it will not last as long as it could. If consumable items are misused they are used up more quickly or wasted. They then have to be replaced sooner than they should be.

? **Which natural resources do you think are used to make paper?**

When we think about all the things we use in school, we soon realise that many of them are shared. This means that the school provides them for people to use at different times. Some of these resources will last for a long time, for example chairs and tables. Other resources are used up more quickly, for example pencils, paper and paints.

Sharing natural resources

The natural resources in a country are, in a way, shared by all the people in a population.

We can take some resources, such as water, for granted. It is easy to think that water is free, but a lot of money is spent cleaning, purifying, distributing and delivering it. Wasting water wastes the money that is spent on providing it.

◀ Salt is taken out of sea water in desalination plants which can be found in many Arabian Gulf countries. Some of this water can be used to grow crops for food.

When food is wasted, it wastes all the resources that have been used to produce it. If food is wasted in a household then that household will spend more money on food than it needs to.

If food is wasted then a country has to spend money buying in more food from other countries.

? **Which natural resources do you think are used to produce food?**

It is important to remember that almost everything uses up resources. There are only limited supplies of some resources, so we need to use those resources especially carefully.

Activities

1 Work in a group to make a list of durable and consumable items in school. Write about how each one should be used.

2 Think of a food you like to eat. Draw and label a diagram showing all the resources that are used to produce that food.

4.4 Using public spaces

In this lesson you will learn:

- why it is important to use public spaces carefully
- how using public spaces carefully is part of being a good citizen.

Public spaces

Public spaces are places that are open and freely accessible by people. Public spaces include streets and pavements, public squares, parks, libraries and beaches.

Other places which are used like public spaces are the halls of shopping malls and waiting areas on public transport systems.

Public spaces in towns and cities are places where people can gather together, meet and relax.

◄ Public spaces are easily reached and can be used by many different people.

Behaviour in public spaces

When we are using public spaces we need to remember that other people are using the same space. So we have to be aware of our behaviour and make sure we do not disturb other people's enjoyment of the place. We should not do anything that would upset or cause offence to others.

? **What behaviour is expected of people in a public library?**

Respecting public spaces

Public spaces are welcome spaces in an urban setting. They are designed to look attractive. How a space looks is partly to do with how clean it is. It is important that people do not throw litter and spoil the look of these places.

Public parks have large areas of grass and beds planted with flowers. They are there for everyone to enjoy and we should not do anything to spoil them.

Public spaces often have seats or benches where people can sit. Some public spaces, such as children's play areas, have special equipment. All of these are shared resources and we should make sure we use them correctly and never do anything to damage them.

▲ It is important to use shared space and shared equipment correctly.

Activity

Work in a group to identify some of the public spaces you know. Write a report about what each space offers and how it should be used.

4.5 The school environment

In these lessons you will learn:
- about different parts of the school environment
- to describe ways in which the school environment is used
- to describe the correct way to treat the school environment.

A primary school environment

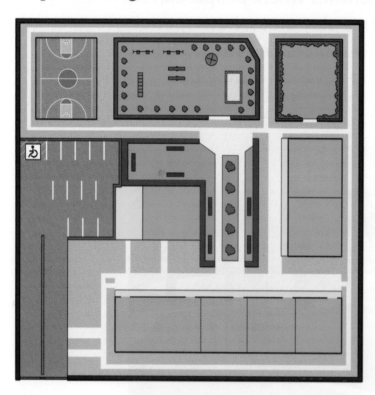

◀ A plan of a primary school.

The plan of a primary school (above) shows the different parts of the school's environment. The land covered by the school has been used in different ways to provide for some of the various needs of the people who use the school.

Areas such as the playground, the courtyard and the garden are like 'public spaces' within the school. These are places where people can meet and talk. They should be attractive spaces that people enjoy being in. Sometimes they have a particular purpose but they are also spaces where people are free to choose what they do. Some people like quiet spaces in which to sit. Some people enjoy running around and being very active.

Inside a school

The floor plan of part of a primary school (below) shows the spaces inside the school. Some of these are like public spaces where people meet and gather together. Other places are 'private' spaces and people cannot simply walk into them or through them. Some of the spaces have a special purpose.

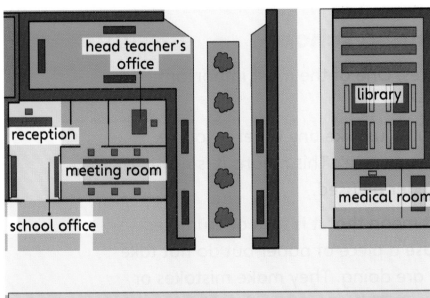

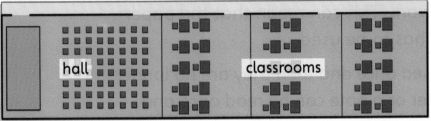

◀ The floor plan of part of a primary school.

Activities

1 Design some outdoor public spaces for your school. Think about some of the different needs of pupils and how your spaces allow for these. Think about how you can make it an attractive place where people want to be.

2 Work in a group to carry out a survey of the different kinds of spaces in your school. Write a report that describes these. List some guidelines to show how the 'public spaces' should be used.

4.6 School resources

Resources and waste in school

A school uses lots of resources. One of the most important resources in a school is paper.

Paper should be used carefully, just like any other resource. Even so, some paper becomes 'waste'. This means it is no longer needed or can no longer be used.

Careless use of paper might mean that it is torn or crumpled. People sometimes start to use a piece of paper but do not take proper care over what they are doing. They make mistakes or do not produce their best work. This can mean that the paper is wasted and a new piece has to be used.

Some pieces of paper are used once and then they are no longer needed. For example, a letter or a note can be read once and then is no longer needed. Old work, notes and files do not need to be stored for very long. These too become waste.

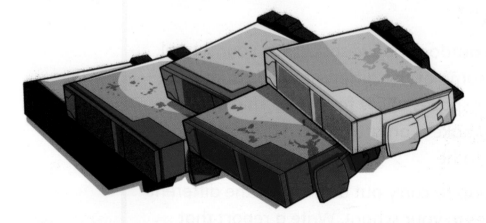

? Schools also use printer cartridges. How can the best use be made of these? What happens to them when they are empty?

It is important to drink a certain amount of water during the day. Water can be brought into school in **disposable** bottles or in **re-usable** bottles. A disposable bottle is designed to be thrown away once it has been used.

▲ A re-usable bottle can be used over and over again.

▲ Disposable plastic water bottles create a lot of waste.

Energy used in schools

The buildings in a school need to be kept at a comfortable temperature. Lights may need to be left on in some rooms and corridors. Meals are cooked and prepared in the school kitchen.

All of this uses a lot of energy.

▲ Turning off electric lights when they are not needed saves resources.

Recycling

Paper, plastics and metals can be recycled. This stops them going into landfill sites and it makes good use of resources.

Activities

1 Work in a group to design a poster that encourages good use of resources in school.

2 Imagine you are a school principal. Write a short letter to parents explaining how recycling happens in school and why you would prefer pupils to bring water in re-usable bottles.

4.7 How do we communicate?

In these lessons you will learn:
- to identify and describe the different ways in which people communicate.

▲ This written verbal communication informs people about the behaviour that is expected of them

What is communication?

Communication is sending and receiving information. Communication can be sent verbally and non-verbally.

Any communication that uses words is called verbal communication. The words can be spoken or they can be written. Spoken communication happens all the time when people talk together. It also happens when people give a presentation, make a speech or perform in a drama.

Communication that does not involve words is called non-verbal. Non-verbal communication can be made using signs and symbols, through art forms such as paintings and sculpture and performances such as dance, mime and music.

People can also communicate using **facial expressions** and **body language**.

Facial expressions

People can communicate a great deal without saying anything at all. They are able to tell a lot from looking at another person's face. Important information is passed by the eyes, mouth and even the eyebrows.

Facial expressions can tell us a lot about what emotions a person is feeling.

▲ How do you think this person is feeling?

Body language

Facial expressions are a part of a person's body language. Body language is to do with how a person's posture and gestures give clues to how they are feeling.

▲ How do you think this person is feeling?

Signs

Signs are used in many situations. They can give people directions, pass on information and give warning of danger. Some signs have words but many do not.

Non-verbal signs using the body

People can use their body to pass on certain types of information or instruction. For example, a person waving might be trying to attract attention, or they may be greeting someone or saying goodbye.
A person can indicate something in particular by pointing at it.

◀ What instruction is this person giving?

▲ What are the different instructions on this panel?

Activities

1 Make a list of the times and ways in which you have communicated today, and the ways in which you have received information.

2 Carry out a survey of examples of communication you see in class, around the school and in your local area.

4.8 Means of communication

In this lesson you will learn:
- to identify and describe different means of communication
- to identify the advantages and disadvantages of different means of communication.

Means of communication

Means of communication are all the devices, items and systems that are used to communicate.

Choosing a means of personal communication

Personal communication takes place between two people or amongst a small group. Speaking face to face is the most direct form and lets those involved receive all the information from facial expressions and body language.

Personal communication takes places through electronic means. People speak using telephones, mobiles and computers. Messages and other information can be shared using email and other messaging services on smartphones, computers and other devices.

Personal communication also takes place when people send physical objects such as letters, cards, gifts and other items through the mail.

▲ People can communicate via computers with others all around the world.

Choosing a means of mass communication

Mass communication happens when a person or an organisation wants to communicate with a large number of people over a wide area. Means of mass communication include newspapers and magazines, posters, radio, television and the internet.

Newspapers, radio, television and the internet can all be used to pass on news and other types of information.

◄ Newspapers are still a popular way for people to keep up with events in their country and around the world.

Companies can use mass communication to **advertise** the things they are making.

Organisations can use mass communications to let people know about what they do or to provide other useful information. An organisation's website lets people know who runs the organisation, what the organisation does and how people can communicate with the organisation.

Activities

1 Write about three different forms of personal communication and say when you would choose each one.

2 Work in a group to identify and write about times when you have received some information through a means of mass communication.

▲ We choose the means we use to communicate depending on who we are communicating with and what we want to communicate.

4.9 Social groups and rules

In this lesson you will learn:
- about different groups to which you belong
- to describe how the different groups operate
- why the groups you belong to have certain rules.

People and groups

People are social. This means that for most of us our lives are spent in groups with other people. We are born into a group. This is our family. We naturally form friendship groups. We find that life is organised around the idea that people live together and meet in groups.

▲ We live our lives surrounded by other people.

Because groups are so important in society it is good to understand what they are and how they work. We should learn how we can be good members of the groups to which we belong.

Social groups

Members of a social group feel they belong to that group. The group is important to them and it is part of their identity. A group's members also work together to achieve a goal. Each member of the group behaves in a way that they would expect other members of the group to behave.

▲ Personal relationships are important in groups of friends and family.

There are usually rules in all groups but they are different depending on the group. In a family, parents tell their children how they expect them to behave. In a group of friends, members understand that the 'rules' are unspoken. We simply expect our friends to behave in a way that will not hurt us or upset us. We expect our friends to be kind.

In more organised groups, such as a school or club, there may be stricter rules. Everyone is expected to obey the rules for the good of the group.

▲ In some groups, behaviour is more closely controlled.

Activities

1 Work in a group to make a list of some groups to which you belong where there are definite rules. Write about who makes the rules and what the rules are for.

2 Write some rules that you think people in a friendship group should follow.

4.10 Public services 1

In these lessons you will learn:

○ about different public services provided in a country

○ to explain the benefits available from public services.

There is a group of people in any country who have the authority to make decisions about what happens in that country. This group of people is called the government.

The government makes **policies** and laws which describe and control the things they want to happen.

The government sets up different organisations to make sure that everything is done.

The government is responsible for providing things that people need.

Education

Governments understand that it is important to provide education in a country. Education lets people develop skills they will need to be able to live in the world. Education also helps people to find out about the world and to develop positive attitudes.

Governments help this by providing buildings such as schools and universities and by training and employing teachers and other staff.

◀ Governments should make sure that modern education facilities are provided in their countries.

Health

If people are healthy, it is good for them as individuals and it is also good for the country. A country has health services to give people the care they need if they are ill or injured. A health service includes buildings such as hospitals, workers such as nurses and doctors, and special transport such as ambulances.

◀ A modern hospital.

The government also spends a lot of time and money informing the public about health issues so that they can make good choices and have the best chance of staying healthy.

Social services

Everyone should be able to have a decent and happy life. Some people within a country need extra help or special care to make sure this happens.

As people get older they may need more care. People who have no family need other people to care for them.

Some people have a disability which means they cannot look after themselves and need extra care and help.

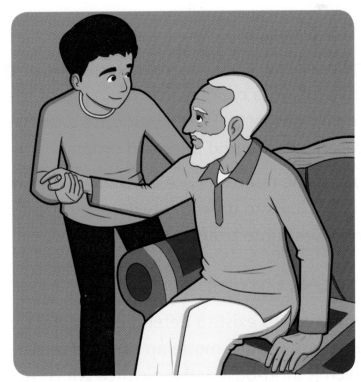

▲ It is right to offer help to people who need it.

Public safety

Governments work to make sure people stay safe by preventing accidents and helping people to avoid becoming unwell.

Public safety is to do with many things. There are rules to do with driving and rules to make sure people are safe when they are working.

Public safety is also to do with making sure that food and drinking water are safe. Food labels have information about when the food should be used. There are rules about what can be added to food.

▲ There are rules about keeping safe at work. Construction workers have to wear special jackets and hats.

The police

The police service is an important part of the system of law and order in a country. The main job of the police is to protect life and property. They investigate crimes, enforce laws, preserve peace and maintain order.

Part of the police service is involved with traffic. The police enforce laws to do with driving, help traffic to flow freely and investigate traffic accidents.

Armed forces

Armed forces exist to defend and protect a country. The armed forces are usually made up of three parts. These are the army, which is land-based, the airforce which uses aircraft, and the navy, which is based on the use of ships and boats.

Transport

Governments are responsible for making sure that people can move around the country quickly and safely. Many of the journeys people make are along roads and highways. There are also public transport systems such as trams, buses and monorails.

▲ Roads are an important part of today's transport network.

The government is also responsible for making sure that people and goods can travel by air and sea to other countries.

Activities

1 Work in a group to gather information about one of the public services provided by the government in your country. Think about buildings and equipment used by the service, people who work in the service, and what the service provides.

2 Write a leaflet describing the public service you found out about in Activity I. Your leaflet should also explain why it is good to have this service.

4.12 Employment

In this lesson you will learn:
- why people need to earn a living
- about different work that people can do.

What is 'work'?

When people work they use their time, energy, skills and talents to produce something. They might produce some things to use themselves and some to sell to other people.

They might work for another person or company. If they do this, we say they are employed. They are given money in exchange for their time, energy, skills and talents.

Why do people work?

People work to satisfy their basic needs for food, shelter and clothing. They work to provide things for themselves and for their family and to improve the way they live.

In some countries people work to make and provide the things they need for themselves. In modern countries most people work to earn money. They then use the money to buy things to meet their needs.

Working can give people a feeling of self-respect because they are able to be independent and to have a sense of achievement.

What sort of work do people do?

Some people work in industries that provide **raw materials**. These are natural resources that can be used in lots of different ways.

▲ Many companies work across the Arabian Gulf region to produce raw materials.

Some people work in industries that make other things out of raw materials. Some materials are processed, or changed, to make them more useful. Other materials are used to manufacture something completely new.

▲ Manufacturing covers everything from making pottery to producing solar panels.

Some people work by providing a service to other people. People pay others to carry out a service for them because they do not have the time or the skill to do it themselves.

▲ People who work in restaurants and hotels provide services for other people.

Activities

1 Work in a group to identify all the different jobs that people do in your community.

2 Think of a job you would like to have. Write about the things you think a person in that job would have to do.

4.13 Consumers

In these lessons you will learn:
- what is meant by the term 'consumer'
- some choices that consumers can make.

People who buy goods and services for their own use are called consumers.

We are consumers because we buy things we need, such as food and clothes, and things to make our lives more comfortable or enjoyable, such as furniture, televisions or holidays.

As consumers we can make choices about what we buy.

Choosing based on price

When people set out to buy goods and services they find that more than one person is selling those goods and offering those services. If the goods or services being offered are exactly the same, the consumer can make a choice based on the price that is being asked. In this case the consumer will probably buy the ones that are cheapest.

Choosing based on value for money

Sometimes a consumer has to decide between goods and services that are similar but not exactly the same. Some of these may be cheaper than others but that does not make them the best ones to buy. Other goods and services may be more expensive but they may also be of a higher quality. More expensive services may be of a higher standard.

◀ High-quality products may last longer than cheaper items of lower quality.

Choosing based on branding

Some goods and services are offered by well-known companies. These companies develop a **brand** which people trust or simply like. Some items are bought because they are **fashionable**.

Choosing based on ethics

Ethics is to do with what a person believes to be right or wrong. Consumers can choose to buy products based on how much those products affect the environment, or whether the people who produce the products receive a fair price.

▲ Companies advertise to encourage consumers to buy their products or services.

▲ Buying food grown locally is good because it will not have been transported far. This uses less fuel which means less harm to the environment.

Activities

1 Carry out a survey of clothes worn by people in your class, and other branded items they own. Find out where they are made. Mark the countries on a world map.

2 Work in a group to find out what kinds of food are advertised most often.

Unit 4 Review questions

1 People who live together in organised communities make up:
   a an institution
   b a society
   c a club
   d a co-operative

2 Honesty and tolerance are examples of a population's:
   a values
   b dreams
   c laws
   d regulations

3 A durable item is one that:
   a can be used in different ways
   b is easily mended
   c should last a long time
   d is made from metal

4 Choose which of these methods of communication uses words.
   a Painting
   b Music
   c Written notes
   d Body language

5 Newspapers, radio and television are all examples of:
   a private communication
   b mass communication
   c personal communication
   d secret communication

6 People who buy goods and services for their own use are called:
   a conductors
   b commuters
   c consumers
   d connectors

7 Write about two ways in which people can help to create a happy and peaceful society.

8 Describe two ways in which people can make the best use of resources in school.

9 Describe the behaviour you would expect people in a friendship group to show towards one another.

10 Identify two public services available in your country and describe what each one offers.

11 Explain briefly why people work and suggest two types of employment people in your country can have.

12 Describe two things that might influence the choice a person makes when buying goods or services.

5 Health and wellbeing

In this unit you will learn:

- how the body uses food
- why exercise is important
- how to stay safe
- about relationships – in the family, at school, among friends
- to draw a useful labelled diagram.

? Which foods do you think help create a healthy diet?

nutrients

body fluids   fibre

organs   infections

joints

5.1 Food and health

In these lessons you will learn:
- how the body uses food
- why it is important to eat well.

Good food

The food we eat contains different nutrients. The body uses these to grow, to maintain and repair itself, and for activity.

There are three main groups of nutrients: carbohydrates, proteins and fats. These three groups provide all the energy the body uses. The body also needs other nutrients called vitamins and minerals, and water to make **body fluids**.

▲ We need to eat different amounts of a variety of foods. The plate shows that most of our food should be fruit, vegetables, cereals and grains.

There two types of carbohydrate: sugars and starches.

- Sugars are simple carbohydrates and your body digests and uses these quickly.

- Starches are complex carbohydrates and it takes your body longer to digest and use these.

Simple carbohydrates are in foods like fruit or yoghurt which also include other nutrients. Foods like sweets and white sugars have no other useful nutrients.

▲ All these foods provide simple carbohydrates but some are better for you than others.

Complex carbohydrates are found in foods like potatoes, wholegrain rice and pasta. These foods also supply other nutrients and something called **fibre**. Fibre helps your digestion and makes you feel full.

Protein helps your body build up muscles and it helps the body repair and look after itself. We get protein from meat, poultry, eggs, dairy products, nuts and legumes (beans, peas and lentils).

Fat is used by the body as a kind of energy store. It helps to protect some **organs** and helps skin and hair to stay healthy.

Fats are in foods from animals and some plant products such as olive oil. It is easy to eat too much fat because the body does not need very much.

Vitamins and minerals do important jobs. They help to make strong teeth and bones and to fight **infections**.

▲ Some processed foods such as fast foods, crisps and cookies have a lot of fat but not many other useful nutrients.

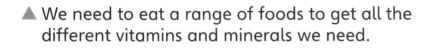

▲ We need to eat a range of foods to get all the different vitamins and minerals we need.

Did you know?

More than two-thirds of your bodyweight comes from water. Every part of you contains water – even your bones.

Activities

1 Draw and write about the foods you eat that give you all the different nutrients you need.

2 Draw and label a meal that you think is good for you. Then draw and label three foods that you think could be called 'treats' or 'luxuries'.

5.2 Exercise and health

In these lessons you will learn:
- how exercise helps to maintain health
- about some problems with modern lifestyles.

Exercise

Eating healthy food is important but your body also needs to move around a lot in order to grow strong and to stay fit.

Your body was made to move about and do things. If you don't exercise, your body starts to slow down, parts of it become weak and you can't move and bend as easily.

Some exercise keeps you fit. Being fit means you are able to be active for longer periods of time. This is called stamina.

Other exercises help to build strong muscles. Strong muscles are important because muscles support your joints and help to prevent injury. They also help you to do things that require strength.

Some exercises help you to be flexible. This means that you are able to bend and stretch.

▲ Exercise helps you to be active for longer, keeps you strong and helps you to stay flexible.

Exercising helps you to sleep better. Getting a good night's sleep is important for concentration and for being in a good mood. When you exercise your body also releases some chemicals called endorphins in your brain that actually make you feel better.

Exercising can also give you time to think and can help you to get rid of bad feelings.

Modern lifestyle

People today have to think about ways in which they can exercise. In the past, people used to walk much more than they do now because people didn't have a car.

There were lots of jobs that needed to be done by hand because there were no machines to do them. People didn't sit in front of televisions and computers because they did not exist.

▲ People spend hours sitting in traffic jams.

◀ There are lots of good things about modern inventions but some of the effects of using them are not so good.

Activities

1 Make a chart and keep a record of all the exercise you actually do in a day.

2 Make a poster explaining the problems of sitting for long periods and encouraging people to exercise more.

5.3 Staying safe at school

In this lesson you will learn:
- where there are problems with safety in school
- to think of ways that people can be kept safe in school.

Accidents in school

Accidents can happen in school as much as anywhere else.

Accidents might be caused as a result of people not following rules or behaving in a dangerous way. Accidents might happen because there is a particular hazard.

An easy way for people to hurt themselves is by falling over. If you fall onto a hard surface then it will hurt and you may injure yourself.

There are ways to make it less likely that you will fall over. For example, you should only run in places where it is safe to do so, and you should always look where you are going.

▲ It is not good to run up and down steps and stairs.

It is important to use any equipment in school in a safe way. Even simple things like pencils or rulers can hurt if they are used carelessly.

Protection from the sun

The sun can damage young skin very easily. In hot, dry countries like those in the Arabian Gulf it can be very harmful. When you are outside you should wear a hat, sunscreen and dark glasses. It is a good idea to wear clothes that cover most of your body.

It is sensible to sit or stand in the shade when that is possible.

Bags and backpacks

Bags and backpacks are useful for carrying things around but they can cause problems.

If you don't wear a backpack properly it can hurt your neck, shoulders and back. Always wear both straps over your shoulders and make sure the backpack is not too heavy.

Keep your bag clean, especially if you carry food in it.

Remember that when you have a backpack on, you are wider than usual! In crowded places it is easy to bump and push into people.

▲ Hats and other headgear can protect you from the sun.

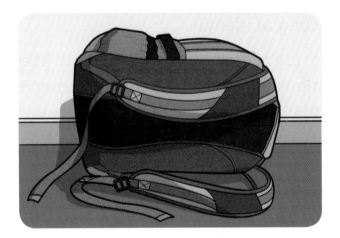

▲ Bag or backpack straps could trip someone up. What is the best thing to do with a backpack when you are not wearing it?

Activity

Work in a group to identify areas around the school that could present hazards.

5.4 Healthy relationships

In these lessons you will learn:

- to identify the important relationships in your life
- why relationships are important
- how to maintain good relationships.

Most people live together with other people and form groups together. Family and other groups often form communities and these combine to create societies. The success of the groups and societies that people create depends on good relationships.

Families and communities

The family is a key part of society. The family provides a feeling of safety and security for its members. It gives them a feeling of identity.

For these reasons it is important to keep relationships within the family strong and healthy. This happens when people in the family show love, respect and care for one another. Older members of a family have a responsibility to set a good example to younger members.

Good family relationships bring happiness to family members, which helps the family stay strong.

▲ Spending time together helps family members build strong relationships.

Groups of families make up communities. It is important for families in these communities to have good relationships. This means that people help and support each other. Sometimes people in a community can work together to bring about something that they want to see happen, or they can offer help to people who need it.

Friendships

Some of our most important relationships are with our friends. We share interests and often think in similar ways. We feel relaxed and comfortable with our friends. Our friends encourage and support us.

▲ Good relationships with our friends help us to be happy.

There will be times when friendships are tested. Friends should be ready to understand each other and to explain their feelings.

Relationships in school

Some of the relationships we have in school are with our friends. We also have to relate to other pupils outside our own friendship groups, and to the adults in the school. We should be kind and show respect to everyone.

▲ Pupils should co-operate with each other and with the adults who work in school.

Activities

1 Write about a group that tries to do something good in your community.

2 Work in a group to make a poster that explains how people can be happy in school.

1 Nutrients are:
   a edible berries found on some trees
   b things our body needs to grow and be healthy
   c special ways of moving
   d food products made from milk

2 Many people today can develop health problems because a modern lifestyle means they:
   a eat too many vegetables
   b read too many books
   c do not get much physical exercise
   d do lots of physical work

3 For a healthy diet people should avoid eating too many foods that are high in:
   a fruit, fibre and nuts
   b sugars, salt and fats
   c cereals, grains and peas
   d fish, cheese and salads

4 It is sensible to wear a hat, sunscreen and sunglasses:
   a at night
   b during a rainstorm
   c in bed
   d when outside in the sunshine

5 Exercising can increase your stamina which:
   a helps you lift heavy weights
   b helps you exercise for longer
   c allows you to bend and stretch
   d helps you run faster

6 Identify three foods that provide us with protein and explain how the body uses protein.

7 Describe two foods we get from animals and two foods that come from plants.

8 Describe two ways in which people can take responsibility for their own health.

9 Describe two ways in which people can try to stay safe in school.

10 Describe three ways in which people should behave towards others in school and say why this behaviour will help to build good relationships.

Glossary

advertise draw attention, through public media, to a product or service

age group a group of people of the same or similar age

agriculture farming, including growing crops and rearing animals for food or other products such as wool

architecture the style in which a building is designed and built

body fluids liquids inside the body, including blood and saliva

body language body movements and postures that express feelings or emotions

brand products made by a particular company, all bearing that company's name

cargo goods carried by ship, aircraft or motor vehicle

chromium a metal used to make stainless steel and for plating to make objects look shiny

cliff a steep rock face, especially on the coast

clues pieces of evidence that lead to a particular thought or idea

community a group of people who live in the same place and who share common characteristics

consumable something that is intended to be used up quite quickly and then replaced

dam a barrier built to hold back flowing water so that it creates a store of water behind it

desalination the process of removing salt from salt water

disposable something that is intended to be thrown away after it has been used

dock an enclosed area of water in a port, designed for loading and unloading ships

drought a long period with very little or no rain, leading to a shortage of water

durable long-lasting and hard-wearing

earth's crust the solid outer layer of the Earth on which we live

ethics to do with what a person believes is right and wrong, sometimes described as 'morals'

expert a person who knows a great deal about a particular subject

facial expressions feelings expressed by movements or the position of features on a person's face

fashionable currently popular

fertile soil that is rich in the nutrients that plants need to grow well

fibre in food, material that is not digested and helps the stomach to feel full

gender male or female

generation all the members of a family or society who are of a similar age

germinate when a seed begins to grow and put out shoots

global relating to the whole world

goods any physical item that people find useful or that they want in order to satisfy a need or desire

habit a way of thinking or acting that a person does without really thinking about it

historian a person who studies what happened in the past

incense a substance that is burned to release a sweet smell

industries different kinds of business that make goods or provide services

infection a disease caused by germs that enter the body

ingredients separate parts that are combined to create something new

irrigation a means of supplying water to growing crops through a system of pipes, channels or tunnels

manufacturing making something, usually on a large scale

monument a building, other structure or site that is of historical interest or importance

nomads people who move from place to place searching out food and water for animals, but having no permanent home

offend to cause someone to feel upset or annoyed

oral spoken rather than written

ore a rock from which a metal can be extracted

organs parts of the body that have a particular function, such as the heart or the liver

peninsula a piece of land projecting out into a body of water. The Arabian Peninsula is also known sometimes as 'Arabia'

policies proposed actions set out by an individual or organisation

prevailing winds winds that are experienced most often in a place

raw materials basic materials from which other things are made

recreation something done for pleasure and enjoyment when not working

resin a thick, sticky substance that is found in some trees and plants

re-usable something that can be used a number of times

ritual a series of actions or a type of behaviour

scrublands land covered with a few small bushes and trees

self-esteem confidence in your own abilities and worth

services help or information provided by one person or company to another person or company

society groups of people living together, usually in the same country or region, and sharing similar ideas, values, laws and traditions

tribe a group that was or is part of a traditional culture whose members are usually linked by family ties

values what is thought to be important in life: 'He valued honesty above everything else.'

Great Clarendon Street, Oxford, OX2 6DP, United Kingdom

Oxford University Press is a department of the University of Oxford. It furthers the University's objective of excellence in research, scholarship, and education by publishing worldwide. Oxford is a registered trade mark of Oxford University Press in the UK and in certain other countries

British Library Cataloguing in Publication Data
Data available

9780198423249

10 9

Paper used in the production of this book is a natural, recyclable product made from wood grown in sustainable forests. The manufacturing process conforms to the environmental regulations of the country of origin.

Printed in India by Gopsons Papers Ltd., Sivakasi

Acknowledgements

The publishers would like to thank the following for permissions to use their photographs:

Cover photo: altrendo travel/Getty, P3: Lebazele/iStock, P13: PIERRE CROM/AFP/Getty Images, P14: Philadelphia Museum of Art/Corbis/Image Library, P15: John Warburton-Lee/AWL Images/Getty Images, P17a: Atlantide Phototravel/Corbis/ Image Library, P17b: Jeffrey Rotman/Corbis/Image Library, P19: © Finnbarr Webster / Alamy Stock Photo, P21: ChameleonsEye/Shutterstock, P23a: Robert Harding Picture Library /Super stock, P23b: Shutterstock.com, P23c: MS Ahmed III 3206 Solon (638-559 BC) Teaching, illustration from 'Kitab Mukhtar al-Hikam wa-Mahasin al-Kilam' by Al-Mubashir (pen & ink and gouache on paper), Turkish School, (13th century) / Topkapi Palace Museum, Istanbul, Turkey / Bridgeman Images, P24: Shutterstock.com, P25: De Agostini/A. Jemolo/De Agostini Picture Library/Getty Images, P26: Roger de la Harpe/Gallo Images/Gettyimages, P27: Nils Kramer/Getty images, P28: age fotostock / Alamy Stock Photo, P29: Zeljkodan/Shutterstock, P31: Merlin74 / Shutterstock.com, P33: Michele Falzone/ JAI/Corbis/ Image Library, P34: Witold Kaszkin/123RF, P42: Allan Baxter/Photolibrary/Getty Images, P43a: Westend61/Gettyimages, P43b: Richard du Toit/Corbis/Image library, P43c: Iain Masterton/Alamy, P44: Patryk Kosmider/Shutterstock, P45a: Joeborg/Shutterstock, P45b: Jochen Tack/arabianEye/Corbis/ Image Library, P45c: shutterstock.com, P51: Piskunov/iStock, P52: James Mackintosh/Alamy, P53: SCIENCE PHOTO LIBRARY, P55a: Richard Allenby-Pratt/arabianEye/Getty Images, P55b: Ali Kabas/Corbis/Image Library, P57a: Rudy Sulgan/Corbis/Image Library, P57b: JOHN KELLERMAN / Alamy Stock Photo, P58: Hung Chung Chih / Shutterstock.com, P65: Iain Masterton/incamerastock/Corbis/Image library, P66: Bibiphoto / Shutterstock.com, P67: Hinnamsaisuy /Dreamstime.com, P69: Kami/arabianEye/Getty Images, P71a: Tanuki Photography/E+/Getty Images, P71b: Pra_zit/Shutterstock, P72: Monique Jaques/Corbis/Image Library, P83: Anne-Marie Palmer / Alamy Stock Photo, P84: Clint McLean/Corbis/Image Library, P85: Philipus / Alamy Stock Photo, P86: Kevpix/Alamy, P87: Fotog/Tetra Images/Corbis/Image Library, P88: Jason Larkin/ arabianEye/Getty Images, P89: KARIM SAHIB /AFP/Getty Images, P90: ShortPhotos/Shutterstock, P91: Harry K Williams / Alamy Stock Photo, P93: Madaland2/Shutterstock, P97: Izzet Keribar/Lonely Planet Images/ Getty Images

Illustrations by Six Red Marbles